How To Get Answers Every Time You *Worship*

By: Dr. R. Buffer

How To Get Answers Every Time You Worship

Published by Interfaith University Press in conjunction with AMC Consultants

© Copyright 2020 Dr. R. Buffer

All Rights Reserved. This book or parts thereof may not be reproduced in any form, stored in any retrieval system, or transmitted in any form by any means- electronic, mechanical, photocopy, recording or otherwise- without prior written permission of the publisher, except as provided by United States of America copyright law. For permissions requests from the author, write to the publisher.

Thank you, Father, for teaching me, in practical ways, ***the power of partnership.***

Table of Contents

Preface……………………………………vii

What is Agreement?………………………1

Prayer and Worship………………………23

IT!………………………………………37

God's Will………………………………67

Covenants………………………………77

Impartation………………………………89

Hymn Song Story: *I Surrender All*………99

Prayers and Confessions…………………109

A Prayer for Our Government……………111

A Prayer for Our Schools…………………115

A Prayer for Revival……………………121

Understanding Redemption..............................127

Understanding Confession……….....................131

A Confession To Walk in the Anointing…........137

A Confession of Praise and Worship…………...143

Your Opportunity to Partner............................149

The Blessing of the Twice Sown Seed…..........151

Becoming A Partner...155

Prayer for Our Ministry Partners…..................159

Preface

How To Get Answers Every Time You Worship has been written for personal enjoyment, interpersonal development, and edification, as well as a reference guide, and/or a study course on the Biblical principles of worship. It is not necessarily designed to be read in one sitting from cover to cover. It can be used for individuals or as a small group's Bible study course (single's group, praise and worship team, prayer team, etc.). It can also be used as a personal daily devotional.

The book is not necessarily designed to be read in one sitting. It is designed to assist you in times of personal *and* corporate worship. In this way, the book can be used as a reference guide. It can also be used as a personal daily devotional. The resource is designed to further the purpose of Singleness of Heart Ministries International: teaching unmarried women to maximize their intimacy with the Lord through a lifestyle of worship. The goal of this resource is to teach women *how* to get answers from God every time they worship.

We'd like to suggest that you set a time and find a quiet place where you will not be disturbed or interrupted as you read each day- a time and place where you can totally focus on your lesson in an atmosphere of worship and reverence for God. If this text is being used as a course for a single's ministry Bible study group or a praise and worship team, we suggest that the group session be held in an area where the group will not be distracted, where an atmosphere of worship may be maintained, and worship sessions can follow the Bible study to implement the lessons that are taught from the group study session. It is suggested that the study group meet at least once a week and cover one chapter per week. In each case, whether the book is used for personal or corporate use, begin each study session by praying that God would minister to you and through you and all persons included. When reading we suggest that you:

1. **Begin with prayer.**

2. **Read the lesson.**

3. **Prayerfully and carefully study each Scripture reference until you understand its meaning and how it relates to the lesson.**

4. Give participants an opportunity to share what they have learned or to ask questions they may have from the lesson.

5. Close with praise/worship, prayer, and confessions of faith from the truths found in that day's lesson.

Simply put, your purpose for reading this book should be to learn how to get answers every time you worship God. So, make a quality decision to implement the principles that you learn immediately after you study each day. Practicing the discipline of immediately implementing the revelation received will help you maintain what you learn from each session. So, implement immediately and meditate frequently on the principles learned and the lessons read.

WHAT IS AGREEMENT?

"Assuredly I say unto you, whatsoever you bind on earth shall be bound in heaven and whatsoever ye shall loose on earth shall be loosed in heaven. Again I say unto you that if two of you shall agree on earth as touching anything that they shall ask, it shall be done for them of my father which is in heaven." Matt. 18:18-19

One thing that many people do not have is a revelation on the *true power of worship*. True worship! The word worship does not refer to just *lip service* or simply *singing a song*. Nor does it refer to singing today's most popular Christian songs or focusing on a new style of singing. There are several Biblical terms that relate to worship, which will be discussed in this study. But simply put, *worship,* refers to our *prostrating* ourselves before God- reverencing God.

Worship is not only important; worship is *revolutionary*! Worship changes things. Through this book you will learn how, through worship, believers can gain the mind of Christ. You will learn how worship changes our perspective and helps us to see things from God's perspective. It is through worship that we get into a posture of agreement- agreement with God.

Amos 3:3 (KJV)-- Can two walk together, except they be agreed?

To agree comes from the Greek word **sumphoneo** **(soom-foe-neh-oh),** **sum** meaning **together** and **phoneo,** meaning *to sound.* **Sumphoneo** means *to sound together, to be in symphony, to be in accord, to be in harmon*y. Glory to God! Metaphorically, sumphoneo, means *to agree together in prayer, to agree with God,* or *sound together with God.* This is such a vital key to worship, as we will later discuss.

The verses in Matthew 18:18-19 deal with the power that the church has to call Heaven on Earth. Glory to God! Let's say that again: You have the power to call Heaven to Earth! Whether in your prayer closet or in the presence of others, you have the power to agree with Heaven and call it into existence here on Earth. Let's look back at verse 18.

Matthew 18:18 (KJV)-- Verily *I say unto you, Whatsoever ye shall bind on earth shall be bound in heaven: and whatsoever ye shall loose on earth shall be loosed in heaven.*

Every time we enter into prayer and begin to praise and worship God, we have a right to hear from God. So, still yourself and listen. *What is the song He is filling your heart with? What is the message God is trying to release?* According to

Matthew 18:18, even through worship, you can use your mouth to loose that message into the Earth and into the lives of His people!

Whatsoever... you bind...*whatsoever* you loose, Heaven will *agree* with. When the church prays, results manifest. Why? Because you are praying *His* mind, *His* Will. You are allowing the Holy Spirit to speak things into existence- even through song form! Hallelujah!

Do you know that there are more than **60 categories of blessings** that Christ died for us to experience? So, open your mouth! He will fill it! Allow *His praise,* His message, His truth to be in your mouth (Psalm 34:1). Receive the blessings that are waiting for you in worship. Don't wait! Do it now!

> **Isaiah 55:6-13 (KJV)--** *Seek ye the LORD while he may be found, call ye upon him while he is near: Let the wicked forsake his way, and the unrighteous man his thoughts: and let him return unto the LORD, and he will have mercy upon him; and to our God, for he will abundantly pardon.* **For my thoughts are not your thoughts, neither are your ways my ways, saith the LORD.** *For as the* **heavens are higher than the earth, so are my ways higher than your ways, and my thoughts than your thoughts.** *For as the rain cometh down, and the snow from heaven, and returned not thither, but watereth the earth, and maketh it bring forth and bud, that it may give seed to the sower, and bread to the eater:* **So shall my word be**

that goeth forth out of my mouth: **it shall not return unto me void,** *but it shall accomplish that which I please, and it shall prosper in the thing whereto I sent it.*

The carnal mind is enmity against God. Man's natural thoughts are lower than God's thoughts. His ways are lower than God's ways. But the good news is we can gain God's mind.

1 Corinthians 2:9-12, 14, 16 (KJV)-- *But as it is written,* **Eye hath not seen, nor ear heard, neither have entered into the heart of man, the things which God hath prepared for them that love him. But God hath revealed them unto us by his Spirit:**

Worship is a *vehicle* of prayer. Glory to God! When we enter worship, the Holy Spirit begins to impress something upon our hearts. The following verses explain, why this is so.

1 Corinthians 2:9-12, 14, 16 (KJV)-- *For what man knoweth the things of a man, save the spirit of man which is in him? even so the things of God knoweth no man, but the Spirit of God.* **Now we have received, not the spirit of the world, but the spirit which is of God; that we might know the things that are freely given to us of God.** *But the natural man receiveth not the things of the Spirit of God: for they are foolishness unto him: neither can he know them, because they are spiritually* discerned. *For who hath known the mind of the Lord, that he may instruct him?* **But we have the mind of Christ.**

This is a faith profession every believer should make constantly: ***I have the mind of Christ!*** This, in essence, meaning *I am in partnership with God; and He reveals His Will, His mind, His thoughts to me as His partner! I am in agreement with God for His Will to be done on Earth. So, I open my mouth to release it!* Glory to God! Let's go back to Isaiah 55 again and specifically look at verses 6-13.

Isaiah 55:6-13 (KJV)-- ***For ye shall go out with joy, and be led***

forth with peace: the mountains and the hills shall break forth before you into singing, and all the trees of the field shall clap their hands. *Instead of the thorn shall come up the fir tree, and instead of the brier shall come up the myrtle tree: and it shall be to the LORD for a name, for an everlasting sign that shall not be cut off.*

This brings me to a particularly important point that must be addressed. All of creation is praising God! When we open our mouths and release God's praises, we are sounding together with Heaven and the universal praises of Earth in united praise unto God.

Many Scriptures reveal that not only do humans sing praise hymns to the Lord; but His material creations sing as well! According to Scripture, trees sing out and creak at the presence of the Lord (1 Chronicles 16:33), stars sing, and angels rejoice, play trumpets, offer incense and gather around the throne of God (Job 38:4-7, Isa. 6, Rev. 8). Psalms 19:1-3 explains that the very heavens declare the Glory of God, "... *Day unto day uttereth speech, and night unto night sheweth knowledge. There is no speech nor language, where their voice is not heard.*" There is a universal praise song, a universal song of worship that *anyone* can understand and everyone who is sensitive to the Spirit of God can hear. Glory to God! It is a song of praise, of worship, of surrender to the Most High God!

When we offer this song in worship to the Lord, it is possible to receive wisdom from God about His Will for our individual lives. But first, we have to get in agreement with Him, asking that His Kingdom come, and His Will be done; and receive it (Matthew 6)! Praise God!

The Bible commands us to "*...forget not all of His benefits....*" There is a survey that reported that 80% of the people in church (whose purpose, as it was with the case of Christ, is to be like God our Father) are dying- spiritually, physically, mentally, socially, and yes, even financially. So, we need to go back and look at the definition of the word "saved;" and answer the question, *"Saved from what? ...Sin?"*

Romans 10:9 (KJV)-- *That if thou shalt confess with thy mouth the Lord Jesus, and shalt believe in thine heart that God hath raised him from the dead, thou shalt be saved.*

This word *saved* actually means *delivered, protected, healed, preserved, to do well, be made whole.* This means when we give our lives to Christ, we should realize that God does not do a half job. Not only does He save us from sin; but Christ died to make us whole- body, soul, and spirit! Jesus came to bind up the brokenhearted- not to fix *one part* and *leave the rest broken.*

So, it is our responsibility to agree with Heaven and *to sound with Heaven.* Hallelujah! The beautiful thing about prophetic worship is that after we have entered His courts with praise and we reach a certain level in praise, we then enter into a holy place of worship. Usually, it is in this place, on this spiritual plane, that the Lord releases His wisdom to us. He gives answers from His Presence concerning the details of our lives. When we acknowledge Him in all our ways, He promised to and *will* direct our path (Proverbs 3:6).

So never forget Satan's tactics of distraction and diversion. Never forget, it is Satan's job is to control you and tempt you not to believe in the atonement of Christ. The reason that 80% of the people in church do not pray is because they feel *"...there is no use in disciplining or afflicting themselves to try to talk to a God that does not provide"*. This is the subconscious thought in the hearts of men; and as a result of thinking this way, 80% of those approaching God through church attendance *cannot* experience the free flow of the blessings that God has so wondrously laid out for them! LORD JESUS! HELP US! Thus, we can't agree on what God says because, many times, *we don't know.*

Hosea 4:6 (KJV)-- *My people are destroyed for lack of knowledge: because thou hast rejected knowledge, I will also reject thee, that thou shalt be no priest to me: seeing thou hast forgotten the law of thy God, I will also forget thy children.*

The Bible says in **Hosea 4:6** that God's people are destroyed, not because Satan is so powerful, not because they are to be so afflicted, broken, ragged, or pious; but because of *a lack of knowledge!* It's time for us to learn the benefits of salvation in the fullness of the revealed knowledge of the Scriptures. Let's look at Acts Chapter 10.

Acts 10:1-9 (KJV)-- There *was a certain man in Caesarea called Cornelius, a centurion of the band called the Italian band, A devout man, and one that feared God with all his house, which gave much alms to the people, and prayed to God alway. He saw in a vision evidently about the ninth hour of the day an angel of God coming in to him, and saying unto him, Cornelius. And when he looked on him, he was afraid, and said, What is it, Lord? And he said unto him, Thy prayers and thine alms are come up for a memorial before God. And now send men to Joppa, and call for one Simon, whose surname is Peter: He lodgeth with one Simon a tanner, whose house is by the sea side: he shall tell thee what thou oughtest to do. And when the angel which spake unto Cornelius was departed, he called two of his household servants, and a devout soldier of them that waited on him continually; And* *when he had declared all these things unto them, he sent them to Joppa. On the morrow, as they went on their journey, and drew nigh unto the city, Peter went up upon the housetop to pray about the sixth hour.*

Acts 10:19-23 (KJV)-- *While Peter thought on the vision, the Spirit said unto him, Behold, three men seek thee. Arise therefore, and get thee down, and go with them, doubting nothing: for I have sent them. Then Peter went down to the men which were sent unto him from Cornelius; and said, Behold, I am he whom ye seek: what is the cause wherefore ye are come? And they said, Cornelius the centurion, a just man, and one that feareth God, and of good report among all the nation of the Jews, was warned from God by an holy angel to send for thee into his house, and to hear words of thee. Then called he them in, and* *lodged them. And on the morrow Peter went way with them and certain brethren from Joppa accompanied him.*

Acts 10:33b (KJV)-- *Now therefore are we all here present before God, to hear all things that are commanded thee of God.*

What a beautiful passage of Scripture! There are certain characteristics in Cornelius' life that identifies that he was a worshiper. Verse two says that he was devout or pious, giving to those who were less fortunate. Another key indicator is seen by what the verse says next: he prayed to God *continually*. He prayed and gave, so much so, that an angel of God appeared to him and told him that his prayers and alms had ascended as a memorial before God. *Lord help us to pray in this same manner!*

In order to accomplish God's will for our lives, we must be dedicated to constantly surrender our lives to God through prayer and worship. We need to begin to pray and worship God give like never before, until our prayers reach heaven- building a memorial before God as Cornelius' prayers did. Then God will connect us with a Peter that has prepared himself through prayer for the Glory of God. There will be an exchange of anointing and power that will fall on us as the Holy Ghost fell on Cornelius and his house (Acts 2:38- 39). Then the miracles and benefits we have read about in this passage of Scripture will become an unmistakable, unquestionable reality in our personal lives!

PRAYER AND WORSHIP

"After this manner therefore pray ye: Our Father which art in heaven, Hallowed be thy name. Thy kingdom come. Thy will be done in earth, as it is in heaven. Give us this day our daily bread. And forgive us our debts, as we forgive our debtors. And lead us not into temptation, but deliver us from evil: For thine is the kingdom, and the power, and the glory, for ever. Amen." Matthew 6:9-13

Before we go any further, let's define the word *pray*. There are several Hebrew and Greek terms that have been translated as either pray or prayer. However, the word *pray*, used by Jesus in the text above, comes from the Greek word **proseuchomai** (pros-yoo-khom-ahee). The word is progressive, starting with the noun *euche*, which means *a prayer to God* and has also been translated as *making a vow*. The word expands to the verb *euchomai*, a special term which means *to make an invocation, request or entreaty*. Adding the prefix, *pros,* which means *in the direction of God*, **prossechomai** becomes the most frequent word used for *prayer*. We will discuss **prossechomai in** more detail later in this chapter. But first, let us look closer at the word euchomai.

It is when looking at the definition of this word, **euchomai**, which means *to make an invocation,* that we will find the power of agreement. Do you remember in Genesis 11, when the unity of the people caused God to take notice of what was going on at the Tower of Babel, to come down to stop the work, and to confuse the languages? Let's look at this passage of Scripture.

> **Genesis 11:1-9 (KJV)--** *And the whole earth was of one language, and of one speech. And it came to pass, as they journeyed from the east, that they found a plain in the land of Shinar; and they dwelt there.* ***And they said one to another, Go to, let us make brick, and burn them throughly. And they had brick for stone, and slime had they for morter. And***

they said, Go to, let us build us a city and a tower, whose top may reach unto heaven; and let us make us a name, lest we be scattered abroad upon the face of the whole earth. And the LORD came down to see the city and the tower, which the children of men builded. And the LORD said, Behold, the people is one, and they have all one language; and this they begin to do: and now nothing will be restrained from them, which they have imagined to do. Go to, let us go down, and there confound their language, that they may not understand one another's speech. So the LORD scattered them abroad from thence upon the face of all the earth: and they left off to build the city. Therefore is the name of it called Babel; because the LORD did there confound the language of all the earth: and from thence did the LORD scatter them abroad upon the face of all the earth.

Take a look at what *unity* did! Unity at work brings God's presence down! This is an example of how unity was used for negative or ungodly purposes. Now, let's look at this principle from the positive. On the Day of Pentecost, they were all together *with one accord* and God's presence came down again!

> **Acts 2:1-11 (KJV)--** *And when the day of Pentecost was fully come, they were all with one accord in one place. And suddenly there came a sound from heaven as of a rushing mighty wind, and it filled all the house where they were sitting. And there appeared unto them cloven tongues like as of fire, and it sat upon each of them. And they were all filled with the Holy Ghost, and began to speak with other tongues, as the Spirit gave*

them utterance. And there were dwelling at Jerusalem Jews, devout men, out of every nation under heaven. Now when this was noised abroad, the multitude came together, and were confounded, because that every man heard them speak in his own language. And they were all amazed and marvelled, saying one to another, Behold, are not all these which speak Galilaeans? And how hear we every man in our own tongue, wherein we were born? Parthians, and Medes, and Elamites, and the dwellers in Mesopotamia, and in Judaea, and Cappadocia, in Pontus, and Asia, Phrygia, and Pamphylia, in Egypt, and in the parts of Libya about Cyrene, and strangers of Rome, Jews and proselytes, Cretes and Arabians, we do hear them speak in our tongues the wonderful works of God.

Unity at work directed toward God for negative or positive will get God's attention. As believers, we have unity. If you have been born again, you have been united with other believers into the Family of God. The key is to learn from the Word of God how to *work that unity* for the positive, productive reasons God gave it to you! It is not enough to simply say we have unity. Unity must be activated in the direction toward God!

Unity is also vitally important in corporate worship settings. Unity is the fundamental principle that the basics of singing- such as *singing on one accord, singing in unison,* and *singing in harmony* are all founded upon. Unity is the place where God commands the blessing (Ps. 133). It is where the anointing shows up, where it dwells. So, in order to live, sing, worship, or do anything in the anointing, we most always endeavor to keep the unity (Eph. 4:3). When we do this, we make room for and welcome the Glory of God and answers from His Holy Presence.

2 Chronicles 5:11-14 (KJV)-- *And it came to pass, when the priests were come out of the holy place: (for all the priests that were present were sanctified, and did not then wait by course: Also the Levites which were the singers, all of them of Asaph, of Heman, of Jeduthun, with their sons and their brethren, being arrayed in white linen, having cymbals and psalteries and harps, stood at the east end of the altar, and with them* *an hundred and twenty priests sounding with trumpets:)* **It came even to pass, as the trumpeters and singers were as one, to make one sound to be heard in praising and thanking the LORD; and when they lifted up their voice with the trumpets and cymbals and instruments of musick, and praised the LORD, saying, For he is good; for his mercy endureth for ever: that then the house was filled with a cloud, even the house of the LORD; So that the priests could not stand to minister by reason of the cloud: for the glory of the LORD had filled the house of God.**

Again, worship is not just about singing. Worship goes much deeper than that. Worship is not just the songs we sing, or *how we sing* the songs that we sing. It is not a style of singing. It is a lifestyle that we offer to God- of *surrender* and *agreement* to His will. This is important not only as it pertains to personal times of worship, but also to corporate worship services. When we worship on one accord, the glory of God is released! Lives are changed! Answers are released! Hallelujah! We must understand that true worship is not about how we sing before others. It is a *way of life* where we surrender obediently to God- taking the back seat, giving God the center stage, *and* total control of our lives.

It is a disposition of reverence and submission to God. So, when we prostrate ourselves before God and reverence God in prayer, guess what!?!

We are worshipping! You see, prayer, praise, and worship go hand in hand. Let's prove this by taking another look back at the scriptural words translated as *prayer* in Scripture.

It is very interesting that in the Old Testament, the Hebrew word, *tephillah (H8605)*, which can be translated by implication as *a hymn* is also seen translated in *over 50* Scriptures as *intercession, supplication* or **prayer**! *Glory to God!* Next let's look back at the Greek word, *proseuchomai*, and at what Jesus said about prayer in the book of Matthew Chapter 6.

> **Matthew 6:5-8 (KJV)--** *And when thou prayest (proseuchomai*

G4336), thou shalt not be as the hypocrites are: for they love to pray standing in the synagogues and in the corners of the streets, that they may be seen of men. Verily I say unto you, They have their reward. But thou, when thou prayest, enter into thy closet, and when thou hast shut thy door, pray to thy Father which is in secret; and thy Father which seeth in secret shall reward thee openly. But when ye pray, use not vain repetitions, as the heathen do: for they think that they shall be heard for their much speaking. Be not ye therefore like unto them: for your Father knoweth what things ye have need of, before ye ask him.

The Greek word used in this passage for pray, prayer, and prayest is proseuchomai. We looked earlier at the various Greek words that make up the word prossechomai- *euche* (a prayer to God), *euchomai* (to make an invocation), and *pros* (in the direction of God). Let us now look again at the word prossechomai. Prossechomai combines these definitions; and can also not only be translated as to pray, but also as to supplicate, and . . . to *worship*. So, *worship* is not just a vehicle of prayer. Worship *IS* prayer! That's right! Worship is prayer; and the deeper we go in worship (prayer) in our secret place, the greater the anointing that we walk in openly.

IT!

"Therefore I say unto you, What things soever ye desire, when ye pray, believe that ye receive them, and ye shall have them." Mark 11:24

Now let's deal with *IT*! One of the reasons many praying Christians have unanswered prayers is the *IT*! Some are praying for *IT* and *IT* does not come. Why? Because *IT* must not only be in unity with a person on Earth, but it also must be *loosed* from heaven. The following process will get you anything you need (Philippians 4:19), want (Psalms

23), or desire from God (Psalms 37:4). It is the Father's good pleasure to give you the kingdom! So, let's discuss practical steps to receiving *IT!*

1. Analyze the Situation. Find out what your needs are, what your debts are, what your sickness is, or what the fear is about. Find out *how much* of *IT* you will need to sustain yourself, your family and the House of God.

2 Corinthians 13:5 (KJV)-- *Examine yourselves, whether ye be in the faith; prove your own selves. Know ye not your own selves, how that Jesus Christ is in you, except ye be reprobates?*

We must ask God to help us know ourselves, so we are not asking amiss!

2. **Research God's Remedy.** Just as you would ask your pharmacist or doctor which medication is best for a specific problem, ask the Great Physician to show you in His written Word what the cure is in your situation. Ask God for His perspective. Then search and research the Bible until you have allowed the Holy Spirit to convince you of an important truth. Christ has redeemed you from the curse of the law! You are redeemed from sin, sickness, debt, fear, lack, sin, etc.!

Galatians 3:13 (KJV)-- *Christ hath redeemed us from the curse of the law, being made a curse for* *us: for it is written, Cursed is every one that hangeth on a tree*:

3. Ask, Seek, Knock. Mark 7:7 and Luke 11:5-8 explains that we are to *ask, seek, knock,* and then *receive*! Yes! Once we know the Will of God (based on His Word) and begin to confess it boldly and consistently, God *hastens His Word to perform it*!

In Luke 11:5-8, we find a parable of a man who went at midnight to his friend asking for bread because he had nothing to give a visitor to his home. Although the friend tried to refuse him, verse 8 explains that his *importunity*, his *shamelessness*; his *persisting in the face of adversity* and refusing to take a denial got him what he requested! Glory to God!

Luke 11:8 (KJV)-- *Though he will not rise and give him, because he is his friend, yet because of his importunity he will rise and give him as many as he needeth.*

Now let's look at Luke 18.

> **Luke 18:1-8 (KJV)--** *And he spake a parable unto them to this end, that men ought always to pray, and not to faint; Saying, There was in a city a judge, which feared not God, neither regarded man: And there was a widow in that city; and she came unto him, saying, Avenge me of mine adversary. And he would not for a while: but afterward he said within*

himself, Though I fear not God, nor regard man; ***Yet because this widow troubleth me, I will avenge her, <u>lest by her continual coming</u> she weary me. And the Lord said, Hear what the unjust judge saith. And shall not God avenge his own elect, which cry day and night unto him, though he bear long with them?*** *I tell you that he will avenge them speedily...*

This indicates that we should be consistently persistent in prayer- growing in intensity and faith until the Master of the house gets up and grants our request! How continual are we in our devotion and worship? How consistent, how heartfelt are our prayers? Efficient prayers (prayers that accomplish much) are heartfelt, persistent, dynamic, and have tremendous power! In this parable, it is clear that the judge was not afraid of this widow woman. Nor did he not grant her request because of personal favoritism. To the contrary, the judge described her as a bother. It was not because of his reverence for God or man. It was due to her persistent character. It was her continual coming (vs. 5). To which the Lord replied, *"Shall not God avenge his own elect, which cry (shout) day and night unto him...."*

How do we have tremendously powerful worship— worship that makes God come down and see what we are doing (Gen 11:1; 1Kings 8:10, 54; 9:1-3)? Hallelujah! It is this type of worship, Scripture explains, that the Lord loves to inhabit.

How is our tehillah (our intercession, supplication, hymns, or prayers) made tremendously powerful? It is through persistence and by the power of the Holy Spirit that our devotion is powerful. Through the discipline of steadfast endurance (consistently worshiping Him in our secret place) we receive this desire (Heb 10:36, 11:6).

4. Partner. If you are saying, "*...I ask, I seek, I knock, but I still can't seem to get my breakthrough,*" you need to bring in the atomic bomb- *partners*! When it seems as though you have reached your faith limit, remember that there are other saints that have conquered this level of negative force; and you have access to their faith through the power of agreement!

James 5:14-16 (KJV)-- *Is any sick among you? let him call for the elders of the church; and let them pray over him, anointing him with oil in the name of the Lord: And the prayer of faith shall save the sick, and the Lord shall raise him up; and if he have committed sins, they shall be forgiven him. Confess your faults one to another, and pray one for another, that ye may be healed. The effectual fervent prayer of a righteous man availeth much.*

Notice the Bible says, *"call for the Elders of the church."* **There are two principles here that should not be ignored:**

a) **The word elder means *older*, not necessarily in age, but in spiritual maturity!** An elder is at least mature in the area that you are struggling with. However, if you have a problem or weakness, a prayer partner with the same weakness won't help you. Obviously, he/she has not developed to the point that he/she is strong enough to bear your infirmity and his/hers as well! Instead of agreeing *with* God, you will begin to unite *against* God and His Will for you; and will get a Tower of Babel or confusion!

b) Remember that the binding and loosing power is connected to the CHURCH. Make it a rule not to partner in prayer with anybody who is not firmly rooted in a local church (at least not for your deliverance)! It is fine to pray with a person who is not in church that understands that the focus of the prayer is mainly for *their* edification. However, if *you* need strength, you must find *strong* prayer partners (Matthew 18:18-19). If you already have a prayer partner, but there is still a problem, repeat steps one through four, and if all lines are clear, bring in another prayer partner and another and another until you have enough power in prayer to bind the strong man or negative force that is blocking your flow of blessing! Just make sure every prayer partner understands and has done the above things and can agree with you that this *IT* is the Will of God and that He wants you to have *IT* (Mk 11:22-24). Start building your prayer partnership today!

5. Praise and Worship God in Faith and Watch it Manifest. We spoke earlier about asking God for *His perspective*. Praise and Worship is a wonderfully powerful and satisfying way to gain

God's perspective and get answers from God. Let's look at this in action. In the following passage of Scripture, we will see what one should do when he or she is in what looks like to the natural eye or what people would call a *"lose-lose"* or a seemingly *"no hope-in-sight"* situation. I exhort you beloved, observe what the power of true praise and worship can do!

> **2 Chronicles 20:1-4, 14 (KJV)--**
> It *came to pass after this also, that the children of Moab, and the children of Ammon, and with them other beside the Ammonites, came against Jehoshaphat to battle. Then there came some that told Jehoshaphat, saying, There cometh a great multitude against thee from beyond the sea on this side Syria; and, behold, they be in Hazazontamar, which*

is Engedi. And Jehoshaphat feared, and set himself to seek the LORD, and proclaimed a fast throughout all Judah. And Judah gathered themselves together, to ask help of the LORD: even out of all the cities of Judah they came to seek the LORD.

Someone went to Jehoshaphat and told him that the children of Moab, Ammon, and the Ammonites, were coming against him to battle. The Bible said that Jehoshaphat feared, and set himself to seek the LORD, proclaiming a fast throughout all Judah. Then Judah gathered themselves together, to ask help of the LORD. You should read this entire chapter but look at what happened next! It was as if Jehoshaphat was emboldened by the Holy Spirit to declare before the Lord; and to remind himself, the people of Judah, and all of creation *just who the Lord is*. He said, *"Are you not the God in Heaven who ruleth over all Kingdom? Are you not the Almighty One?"* As if to say, *"nothing is too hard for you!"*

Jehoshaphat begins to make confessions declaring God's goodness towards Him and His people, of His faithfulness, of the things He had done. He reminded God of His promise to help His people if they cried unto Him. It was as if he was reminded of his partnership with God and simply called covenant to the carpet by asking God, *"Will you not defend us?"*

Then the Holy Spirit came upon Jahaziel in the midst of the congregation; and he releases the sound of their victory. He prophesies their victory *over* their enemies! What does he say?

2 Chronicles 20:15-19 (KJV)-- *And he said, Hearken ye, all Judah, and ye inhabitants of Jerusalem, and thou king Jehoshaphat,* **Thus saith the LORD unto you, Be not afraid nor dismayed by reason of this great multitude; for the battle is not yours, but God's. Tomorrow go ye down against them: behold, they come up by the cliff of Ziz; and ye shall find them at the end of the brook, before the wilderness of Jeruel. Ye shall not need to fight in this battle: set yourselves, stand ye still,**

and see the salvation of the LORD with you, O Judah and Jerusalem: fear not, nor be dismayed; tomorrow go out against them: for the LORD will be with you.

He tells them not to be afraid because of the multitude. Then he gave them a Word from the Lord, "*. . . The battle is not yours! The battle belongs to the Lord.*" This is what God showed Jehaziel *as they were praying*. So, his faith *spoke!* Jehaziel explains to them the divine strategy that God revealed to Him.

The Bible says in verse, 18 that *"Jehoshaphat bowed his head with his face to the ground: and all Judah and the inhabitants of Jerusalem fell before the LORD, worshiping (laying prostrate) before the LORD. And the Levites, of the children of the Kohathites, and of the children of the Korhites, stood up to praise the LORD God of Israel with a loud voice on high."*

2 Chronicles 20:20-24 (KJV)-- *And they rose early in the morning, and went forth into the wilderness of Tekoa: and as they went forth, Jehoshaphat stood and said, Hear me, O Judah, and ye inhabitants of Jerusalem; Believe in the LORD your God, so shall ye be established; believe his prophets, so shall ye prosper. And when he had consulted with the people, he appointed singers unto the LORD, and that should praise the beauty of holiness, as they went out before the army, and to say, Praise the LORD; for his mercy endureth for ever. And* *when they began to sing and to praise, the LORD set ambushments against the children of Ammon, Moab, and mount Seir, which were come against Judah; and they were smitten. For the children of Ammon and Moab stood up against the inhabitants of mount Seir, utterly to slay and destroy them: and when they had made an end of the inhabitants of Seir, every one helped to destroy another. And when Judah came toward the watch tower in the wilderness, they looked unto the multitude, and, behold, they were dead bodies fallen to the earth, and none escaped.*

The Holy Spirit gave *Jehoshaphat* a Word. After which, He gave him a strategy. Do you know what happened next? He gave Jehoshaphat a *divinely inspired* "right-now" *faith-filled song* (Heb

11:3). And they sung it out! *"...Praise the LORD; for his mercy endureth forever!"* Over and over again, I'm sure they said it. Through praise and worship, they got answers in a life- threatening situation!

The issue is obvious- an impending attack upon Jehoshaphat and Judah. They needed a solution and quick! How did they get an answer? Verse 18 says that Jehoshaphat's response to the problem was to worship before the Lord! Can you believe it? Glory to God! *Oh, how God takes foolish things to confound the wise, the elite, the obvious winner, the bully!* God's used p*raise and worship* to defeat their enemies in a *war!*

Jehoshaphat appointed specific singers to go *before* the army, to *release* victory *before* they *saw* victory. What a "Kingdom of Heaven" strategy! It was a *Kingdom* strategy that won the war. By the time Judah got there everyone was dead. Dead bodies were all over the battlefield. None had escaped! So, as the Lord had promised, there was no need for them to fight (2Chr. 20:15-17). *Glory to God!* The only sacrifice that was required of them was the sacrifice of praise.

It cannot be overstated that one of the most prized aspects of offering sincere praise and then flowing into worship is that it takes us to another *spiritual plane*. We rise in faith emboldened to believe God, to walk by faith. We see what others can't see. So, we say what others wouldn't dare say! In fact, we *boldly* say what God says in the face of adversity! Our faith speaks and we release words of faith that causes other to believe.

Notice, before we go on to the next point, that we also see the aforementioned steps to getting *IT* illustrated in this passage. They analyzed the situation. They sought God for His solution. Then they partnered together, and were persistent in prayer, fasting, praise, and worship.

6. Separate from bad company, negative friends, bad teaching and from preaching that is not in faith in God's total Word.

1 Corinthians 15:33 (KJV)-- *Be not deceived: evil communications corrupt good manners.*

2 Timothy 2:15-18 (KJV)-- *Study to shew thyself approved unto God, a workman that needed not to be ashamed, rightly dividing the word of truth. But shun profane and vain babblings: for they will increase unto more ungodliness. And their word will eat as doth a canker: of whom is Hymenaeus and Philetus; Who concerning the truth have erred, saying that the resurrection is past already; and overthrow the faith of some.*

In this passage of Scripture, Paul warns Timothy to keep away from the fruitless, vain discussions of *Hymenaeus and Philetus*. These men are recorded as being opposers of Christianity. Paul's warning likened the effects of listening to those types of words to the effects of having an ulcer. *My Lord!*

7. If the enemy attacks you with doubt, do it again. Repeat these steps as often as necessary. However, the bottom line is your *IT* must line up with your prayer partner's level of faith *and* the Will of the Father in Heaven. How do we know the Will of the Father? We know, agree, and also pray the Will of the Father according to the Word of Almighty God. If God says *IT*, bank on *IT*. Agree with God! Say what God says and you will truly have *whatsoever* you say (Mk 11:22-24)! The only thing to do now is to determine what is *your IT*?

Matthew 6:31-33 (KJV)-- *Therefore take no thought, saying, What shall we eat? or, What shall we drink? or, Wherewithal shall we be clothed? (For after all these things do the Gentiles seek:) for your heavenly Father knoweth that ye have need of all these things. But seek ye first the kingdom of God, and his righteousness; and all these things shall be added unto you.*

Matthew 6:33 says to *seek first His righteousness* and *then* He will bless you with *IT*!! But how do you seek the kingdom?

1) **Watch and pray for opportunities to sow.** We should give our finances, time, energy, and prayer into an anointed ministry (a ministry with VISION)

that is spreading the Good News of THE KINGDOM OF GOD!

Galatians 6:6 (KJV)-- *Let him that is taught in the word communicate unto him that teacheth in all good things.*

2) **Preach the Word.** Witness to friends and neighbors. Pray about ways to give away tracts, good sound Christian books, audios, and videos. Get the Gospel out any way you can in the Spirit of God.

3) **Put God First.** Stop thinking about how much you can *get* from God; and think about how much you can *do* for God's Kingdom! You may require only a small cramped compact car for yourself, but

the Kingdom of God may call for a minivan to transport people to church. Pray until you find out what God wants you to have because *that* is your true need. Your family may require only a two-bedroom house, but to help some Christian brother or sister, the Kingdom may call for a five-bedroom home.

Seek first the Kingdom of God and His righteousness! It's time to get *IT* right. When you hunger and thirst to do right, and help others, you, in turn will be abundantly blessed! With that being said, someone may ask, *"Should I sow financial seed into any person or any ministry that asks? How do I know where I should sow? Should I sow into anything that looks like it's the Kingdom of*

God?" No. Would you sow one or two or three peas to a field? No!! Of course not. You would have to go to two or three different locations just to get started on one pot of peas!! The bottom line is to sow where:

1) God leads,

2) The ground is good,

3) The Gospel is being preached,

4) Souls are being saved, and

5) Christians are edified.

Matthew 18:19 (KJV)-- *Again I say unto you, That if two of you shall agree on earth as touching anything that they shall ask, it shall be done for them of my Father which is in heaven.*

Do all of this under the anointing or the witness of the Holy Spirit! Pray and worship God. He will direct your path. So, what is your *IT*? Let's agree as touching and *it is done* according to God's Will!

GOD'S WILL

"Faith comes by hearing and hearing by the Word of God." Romans 10:17

We have already established that God's Word *is* His Will. But let's dig deeper!! If you genuinely want to be blessed, you must allow God to really speak to your heart about your need. Then you must validate with Scripture that it is in agreement with His Will for your life that you have *IT*. After that, you must make that Scripture and revealed Word from God your faith!

Hebrews 11:1 in the Amplified Bible reads, *"**NOW FAITH is** the assurance (the confirmation, the title deed) of the things [we] hope for, being the proof of things [we] do not see and **the conviction of their reality** [faith perceiving as real fact **what is not revealed to the senses**].*" So, when we begin to worship God, and receive answers from Him, our faith becomes a conviction of the reality of something that we may not be able to see with our *natural* eyes. Do you know what happens when are hearts are "full to overflowing" with faith? Our faith automatically speaks, and we act on our faith!

Romans 10:8 (KJV)-- *But what saith it? The word is nigh thee, even in thy mouth, and in thy heart: that is, the word of faith, which we preach (herald, proclaim, publish).*

This is why it is so important that we sing songs of faith, songs based on God's Word- not doubt and unbelief. Singing unscriptural songs that glamorize struggle or that say, for example, "climbing up the rough side of the mountain" versus "telling the mountain to be removed and cast into the sea" may be popular in certain circles. But singing these types of songs, first and foremost, is not true worship because it is not in agreement with God's Word. It is simply complaining or rehearsing doubt.

Secondly, singing these types of songs affects our confidence *in* God and *before* God. In order to receive from God, you must first believe that He is and that He is who He says He is. Glory to God!! Spending time in the Presence of the Lord builds our faith- not our doubt. It makes timid songs bold declarations! That's right, *the moment* God makes a word alive in your spirit you *have* faith. Now! As Hebrews 11:1 says, "Now faith!" Let's look at another passage of Scripture that will help us discern if *IT* is according to God's Will.

Mark 11:12-14, 19-21 (KJV)--
And on the morrow, when they were come from Bethany, he was hungry: And seeing a fig tree afar off having leaves, he came, if haply he might find anything thereon: and when he came to it, he found nothing but leaves; for the time of figs was not yet. And Jesus answered and said unto it, No man eat fruit of thee hereafter for ever. And his disciples heard it. And when even was come, he went out of the city. And in the morning, as they passed by, they saw the fig tree dried up from the roots. And Peter calling to remembrance saith unto him, Master, behold, the fig tree which thou cursedst is withered away. And Jesus answering saith unto them, Have faith in God. For verily I say unto you, That whosoever shall say unto this mountain, Be thou removed, and be thou cast into the sea; and shall not doubt in his heart, but

shall believe that those things which he saith shall come to pass; he shall have whatsoever he saith. Therefore I say unto you, **What things soever ye desire, <u>when ye pray</u> believe that ye <u>receive</u> them, and <u>ye shall have them</u>**.

The word that is used in this passage for prayer is also the Greek word, proseuchomai, which again means *to pray to God, supplicate, and worship! This is so powerful!* Hallelujah! So, whenever you enter worship (whether in public or private), you should always be aware of the *desire* that you receive. In other words, pay more attention to the desires you receive from the Holy Spirit *during* prayer verses the desires you receive *prior* to prayer or even *after* prayer.

The desire or unction that we receive from the Holy Spirit *during* worship *is* the signal of what God has released. It lets us know it is time to receive that particular thing! This puts me in mind of a metronome, which is a mechanical or electrical instrument that makes clicking sounds at an adjustable pace. Musicians use it to practice staying *on* rhythm. Similarly, the Holy Spirit is like our metronome, in this regard, keeping us in timing with the Father's Will.

I have a vacuum sealer at home. A vacuum sealer is a device a lot of people use to preserve food. The food is placed in the plastic bag. The open end of the plastic bag is put in the vacuum sealer; and the sealer is used to suck out the air and seal the bag to preserve the food. When my vacuum sealer has completely sealed the bag, a light comes on indicating that the sealing process is completed, and the vacuum sealer has released the bag from the sealing process. The light lets me know I can now take (or receive) the bag.

Likewise, when we receive a desire in prayer, it is like that light indicating it is time to receive the specific thing we are desiring. It is the signal revealing what has been released or granted to us by our Heavenly Father. It is a vivid indication of our Father's Will for us. *What a good, loving Father He is!*

In a worship service, we may be led spontaneously to sing a certain song that we hadn't planned to sing in a new, relevant, and fresh way! This is what is now called "spontaneous worship." This can also happen in times of personal prayer where the Lord may lead us to worship Him with a certain song. He may give us an *impromptu* melody of songs that builds our faith and reminds us of (or gives illumination on) a certain promise in Scripture; and we receive direction from Him. As Romans 10:17 tells us, *faith comes by hearing and hearing by the Word of God.*

COVENANTS

"...I ...will be their God; and they will be my people."
Jeremiah 31:33

From the beginning, God is revealed as the covenant maker. The basic meaning of *"covenant"* in the Bible is summed up in the words of Jeremiah in chapter 31 verse 33: *"I will be their God; and they will be my people."* God enters into a special relationship with men and women. He commits himself to protect His people, and in return he expects obedience from them.

Most covenants in the Bible are between God and man. There are also "man to man" covenants in the Old Testament. The Bible itself is arranged into two major "covenants"-the Old and the New. They are more often called by the synonyms- the Old and New *Testaments*. The Old Covenant is the one made with Moses on Mt. Sinai, when the Ten Commandments were given to God's people as the basic rules for living. This covenant forms the basis for Israel's religion.

There are also other covenants in the Old Testament. There is the one God made with Noah after the flood. This is God's general covenant with all people. Then there is the covenant God made with Abraham (Gen. 15). God promised that his descendants would have a land of their own, and he urged them to share their blessings with the other nations of the earth. This is God's covenant with His special people, renewed in the covenant with Moses at Mt. Sinai.

The New Testament writers show that the New Covenant between God and men (to which the Old Testament looks forward) rests on the death of Jesus. Jesus Himself said *"this cup of the New Covenant, sealed with My blood."* The Book of Hebrews compares the Old and New Covenants. The New Covenant offers something that the Old could never secure- release from the power of sin, and the freedom to obey God. Let's look at one more passage of Scripture.

Genesis 22:1-5 (KJV)-- *And it came to pass after these things, that God did tempt Abraham, and said unto him, Abraham: and he said, Behold, here I am. And he said, Take now thy son, thine only son Isaac, whom thou lovest, and get thee into the land of Moriah; and offer him there for a burnt offering upon one of the mountains which I will tell thee of. And Abraham rose up early in the morning, and saddled his ass, and took two of his young men with him, and Isaac his son, and clave the wood for the burnt offering, and rose up, and went unto the place of which God had told him.* **Then on the third day Abraham lifted up his eyes, and saw the place afar off.** *And Abraham said unto his young men, Abide* *ye here with the ass; and I and the lad will go yonder and worship, and come again to you.*

This is such a powerful Scripture! In verse two, we see that God told Abraham to take his only son, Isaac, to Moriah and offer him as a burnt offering upon one of the mountains. The land of Moriah included all the mountains of Jerusalem-Calvary, Zion, Olive, Moriah, etc.

Mt. Calvary is where Christ was crucified. It is very interesting that God told Abraham to offer Isaac (practically as a type of Christ) in the same area, possibly on the same mountain that Christ offered His life. In Genesis Chapter 15, we see that God made a covenant with Abraham, telling him that his heir would not be a servant, but it would be his own child. Isaac was the heir that God had promised Abraham; and now God was telling Abraham to sacrifice His son of promise!

Verse four says that on the *third* day, Abraham lifted his eyes and found the place afar off. Abraham said unto his men, "...***Abide ye here with the ass; and I and the lad will go yonder and worship, and come again to you.***" Worship, he said. Abraham told the men, "*I and the lad will go yonder and worship and come again to you.*"

Here we see another example element of worship that we discussed in the last chapter, namely- sacrifice. Abraham's faith was speaking.

God said **sacrifice your son** *on one of the mountains in the land of Moriah that I will tell thee of. Abraham said to the men that he and the lad* **were going to worship and were coming again to them**. *Indeed, Abraham's faith was speaking!*

> **Genesis 22:6-8 (KJV)--** *And Abraham took the wood of the burnt offering, and laid it upon Isaac his son; and he took the fire in his hand, and a knife; and they went both of them together. And Isaac spake unto Abraham his father, and said, My father: and he said, Here am I, my son. And he said, Behold the fire and the wood: but where is the lamb for a burnt offering? And Abraham said, My son, God will provide himself a lamb for a burnt offering: so they went both of them together.*

Again, we see a result of Abraham's lifestyle of worship: he could see on another spiritual plane. He did not forget the covenant God made with him. So, when Isaac asked his father, *"...where is the lamb?" Abraham's NOW faith was speaking!* He had absolute confidence in God. Isaac was God's promised son to Abraham and Sarah.

> **Genesis 22:9-14 (KJV)--** *And they came to the place which God had told him of; and Abraham built an altar there, and laid the wood in order, and bound Isaac his son, and laid him on the altar upon the wood. And Abraham stretched forth his hand, and took the knife to slay his son. And the angel of the LORD called unto him out of heaven, and said, Abraham, Abraham: and he said, Here am I.*

And he said, Lay not thine hand upon the lad, neither do thou any thing unto him: for now I know that thou fearest God, seeing thou hast not withheld thy son, thine only son from me. And Abraham lifted his eyes, and looked, and behold behind him a ram caught in a thicket by his horns: and Abraham went and took the ram, and offered him up for a burnt offering in the stead of his son. And Abraham called the name of that place Jehovahjireh: as it is said to this day, In the mount of the LORD it shall be seen.

Abraham begins to sacrifice his son . . . but God stops him! Abraham's actions confirmed what God thought about Abraham. Abraham's intentions were nothing but utter obedience and complete surrender to God's will.

God's response was, *"...Now I know that you fear God seeing you have not withheld your son from me."* His mind was so resolved to sacrifice his son, that God counted even his intentions as complete obedience. Glory to God! This is what a lifestyle of worship produces- complete obedience.

Abraham finds the ram in the bush; and just as the ram was a substitution for Isaac, so Christ became a substitute for all men. This was an Old Testament foreshadowing of the covenant every human being can have with God through accepting Jesus' sacrificial death, who paid the penalty for our sin.

Genesis 22: 15-19-- And the angel of the LORD called unto Abraham out of heaven the second time, And said, By myself have I sworn, saith the LORD, for because thou hast done this thing, and hast not withheld thy son, thine only son: That in blessing I will bless thee, and in multiplying I will multiply thy seed as the stars of the heaven, and as the sand which is upon the sea shore; and thy seed shall possess the gate of his enemies; And in thy seed shall all the nations of the earth be blessed; because thou hast obeyed my voice. So Abraham returned unto his young men, and they rose up and went together to Beersheba; and Abraham dwelt at Beersheba.

Here, we come to understand, that it is Jesus who was sent by the Father, as *"the Angel of*

Jehovah." In verse 16, we see Christ saying, *"...by myself I have sworn (made an oath) to bless Abraham: to make his seed as the stars of the heaven and as the sand of the seashore"*. Because of the covenant God made with Abraham; and because Abraham kept the principle of obedience, God told Abraham that all of the nations of the Earth would be blessed through his seed. What a covenant!

Scripture References: Genesis 9:1-17; 12:1-3; 15:17-21; Exodus 19:6; 20:1-7; Jeremiah 31:31-34; I Corinthians 11:25; Hebrews 8:13; 10:4.

IMPARTATION

For God is my witness, whom I serve with my spirit in the gospel of his Son, that without ceasing I make mention of you always in my prayers; Making request, if by any means now at length I might have a prosperous journey by the will of God to come unto you. For I long to see you, that I may impart unto you some spiritual gift, to the end ye may be established;" Romans 1:9-11

This new covenant gives us a fresh revelation of the character of God; and we perceive that we do not only *seek* the Kingdom of God and His righteousness, but in the Blood, *we find IT!* Hallelujah! The model prayer states, *"Thy will be done on Earth, as it is in Heaven."* In other words, God's will is to bring Heaven to Earth; *and to do so* He makes covenant with man. When men who covenant with God get together, they make up the Body of Christ, the Church, and bring the Kingdom of God on Earth!

I Samuel 18:1-4 NASV-- *Now it came about when he had finished talking to Saul, that the soul of David and Jonathan were knit together and he loved him as himself. And Saul took him that day and did not let him return to his father's house.*

Then Jonathan made a covenant with David because he loved him as himself. And Jonathan stripped himself of the robe that was on him and gave it to David, with his armor, including his sword and his bow and his belt.

Glory to God! What a covenant between two God fearing men! They became unified and agreed to the point that Jonathan took down his defense and joined himself to David. He took his armor off, thus opening himself up to receive whatever David would return to him. David returned love. The armor was the token of exchange which was common among covenant makers in the Bible. Similarly, God gives us protection and provision and we are to respond in loving obedience. In giving David his royal robe, his armor and his sword, his bow and belt, Jonathan was giving to David his authority of succession to his father's throne. Now, let's look at how tokens of exchange were used in the life and ministry of Paul the Apostle.

Acts 19:11-12-- *And God wrought special miracles by the hands of Paul; So that from his body were brought unto the sick handkerchief's or aprons, and the disease departed from them, and evil spirits went out of them".*

Here, once again, we see an object exchanged (**Paul's materials**) as a point of contact (**tokens of**

covenant) to another person who was involved in the impartation.

To **impart** means *to give, share, distribute, grant.* The word implies **liberality** or **generosity**. This is the word used in Scriptures to exhort those with two outer tunics to give one to someone who has none (Luke 3:11); to encourage people to give with a cheerful outflow (Romans 12:8); and to urge workers to labor with industry, in order to give to him who has a need (Ephesians 4:28).

Ephesians 4:7-8 says, *"But unto every one of us is given grace according to the measure of the gift of Christ. Wherefore he saith, When he ascended up on high, he led captivity captive, and gave gifts unto men.*" So, every Christian has a gift in God. Verse 12 says, "…. for the work of the ministry, for the edifying of the Body of Christ."

Writing to the church at Rome, Paul says... "*For I long to see you, that I may **impart** unto you some spiritual gift, to the end that ye may be <u>established</u>*" (Romans 1:11). Here *to impart* means simply *"to give over and to share."* It means to convey from one person to another. The Apostle Paul had the desire to impart to the saints some spiritual gift or spiritual help.

Spiritual impartations are given to help us fulfill the Will of God for our lives. This is part of the equipping. We are equipped to do the work of the ministry through *impartation*. The *result* is *establishment*. The New English Bible says, "to make you strong." The Twentieth Century New Testament says, *"and so give you fresh strength."* So, the believer is equipped with fresh strength as a result of impartation.

Impartation will come often through association. In this way, there will be a transference of anointing *from* or *to* the people you associate with. We can receive through impartation from the ministries we submit to and associate with.

There are certain people whom I believe the Lord has destined you to hook up with in the

Spirit. They will have the spiritual deposits you need. It is not the will of God that we lack any necessary gift, information, materials, or anointing (in manifestation of the Holy Spirit). He has given us the means to obtain all we need. He is ready and willing to equip us with all the grace we need to complete our commission which is to preach the Gospel to all nations and make disciples of men.

If we are lacking, it's not God's fault. So, it is important to associate with strong churches and strong ministries. If you associate yourself with weakness, you will become weak. If you associate with strength, you will become strong. You will become like the people you associate with. Don't allow yourself to become weak by linking up with the wrong kind of people.

Partnership with the appropriate people is important for individuals, businesses, and even for ministries. If you are passionate about preaching or sharing the Gospel through worship or if you are just praying for an impartation to operate in deeper levels of worship, I encourage you to pray about partnering with a ministry that has a revelation on how to maximize intimacy with God through worship. Visit our website, we'd love to partner in prayer with you!

HYMN SONG STORY: *I SURRENDER ALL*

I grew up in the Methodist church, which of course means I grew up singing a lot of hymns. When I was younger, I did not fully appreciate hymns. Now that I am older, I appreciate them so much more: the songs and the story behind the songs. One of my favorite hymns as a child was "I Surrender All". The following is the Song Story of the hymn "I Surrender All".

"I Surrender All" is a Christian hymn, written by Judson W. Van DeVenter and put to music by Winfield S. Weeden, and published in 1896.

Judson W. Van DeVenter was born on a farm in Michigan in 1855. After he attended Hillsdale College, he became an art teacher and supervisor of art in the public schools of Sharon, Pennsylvania. DeVenter was also an accomplished musician, singer, and composer. Van DeVenter, as an active layman in the Methodist Episcopal Church, became very involved in the church's evangelistic meetings. Yet he felt the Lord leading him to do more.

His friends recognized his giftings and urged him to give up teaching to become an evangelist. But Van DeVenter had a strong desire to become a recognized artist. He struggled for five years between the decision of becoming an artist or devoting himself to ministry. Read below Van DeVenter's personal description of the account:

> *"For some time, I had struggled between developing my talents in the field of art and going into full-time evangelistic work. At last, the pivotal hour of my life came, and I surrendered all. A new day was ushered into my life. I became an evangelist and discovered down deep in my soul a talent hitherto unknown to me. God had hidden a song in my heart, and touching a tender chord, He caused me to sing."*

It is said that the song was written while he was conducting a meeting in East Palestine, Ohio at the home of a noted evangelist named, George

Sebring. After he decided to surrender his life to God's call for his life, he traveled extensively throughout the U.S., England, and Scotland evangelizing and visiting art museums along the way. Towards the end of His life, he moved to Florida and was a professor of hymnology at Florida Bible Institute for four years in the 1920s. After retiring, DeVenter reportedly would regularly visit the students on campus and conduct "sing-a-longs."

The power of hymns is so amazing! Who would think that a simple hymn of worship, of surrender could be so impactful? Perhaps the most important (or notable) impartation that this man who chose to surrender made was on a young evangelist by the name of Billy Graham. Yes …*the Billy Graham!*

Billy Graham was a student at Florida Bible Institute. Believe it or not, Rev. Billy Graham cites this specific hymn, *I Surrender All,* as "an influence in his early ministry". His account, which appears in *Crusade Hymn Stories*, edited by Graham's chief musician, Cliff Barrows, reads as follows:

"...One of the evangelists who influenced my early preaching was also a hymnist who wrote 'I Surrender All'- the Rev. J. W. Van de Venter. He was a regular visitor at the Florida Bible Institute

(now Trinity Bible College) in the late 1930's. We students love this kind, deeply spiritual gentleman and often gathered in his winter home at Tampa, Florida, for an evening of fellowship and singing."

This hymn of devotion, *I Surrender All*, epitomizes the ultimate purpose of true worship: surrender to God and His Holy Will. What an effect obedience has, not only on the individual that obeys, but on all who see or hear of the example. A true hymn is a holy, song of praise, full of faith and conviction of a Heavenly truth (revealed by the Holy Spirit) which, once offered unto God in agreement with Heaven, changes things in spiritual and natural realms. Often, they are the by-product produced when one has received answers or direction from the Lord.

Birthed in prayer and released in the form of a hymn, Rev. J. W. VanDeVenter conveyed a powerful truth in the Earth: the need to surrender to God's Holy Will for His life. Rev. Graham's account of DeVenter's last words prior to his passing were that *"...the words of this hymn were the last words DeVenter sang, just above a whisper, when he passed...."* What was birthed out of this one man's worship, in the end, contributed to millions of souls coming into covenant with the Lord Jesus! Hallelujah!

In this hymn, the message is simple: unabandoned surrender. Dr. Michael Hawn, a distinguished professor of church music at Perkins School of Theology, writes this of the hymn:

> *"...Each of the five stanzas begins with the line, 'All to Jesus I surrender.' The refrain includes the phrase, "I surrender all" three times in the melody and an additional two times in the men's part. This means that the one who sings all five stanzas would sing the word 'surrender' thirty times. The other key word – 'all'– would be sung forty-three times!*
>
> *The stanzas all revolve around the key word. Stanza one stresses complete surrender: 'all to him I freely give'. In stanza two, the singer forsakes 'worldly pleasures'. In stanza three, the*

singer prays to 'feel the Holy Spirit'. Stanza four seeks the Lord for empowerment and to be filled with 'thy love and power'. In the final stanza, the singer 'feels the Sacred Flame', a reference to the Holy Spirit. The result of feeling Christ's 'full salvation', is to sing 'glory to his name'."

Under the power of the Holy Spirit, Rev. Judson W. Van DeVenter released a song from his Spirit that expressed the conviction of the answer he had given the Lord. This conviction was to forsake his own plans for the preaching of the Gospel of Jesus Christ, evangelism, and making disciples of every Nation. DeVenter did just that: traveling throughout the world as an evangelist. This song released out of mouth, born out of prayer, changed things in spiritual and natural realms. Who knows how many millions of souls sang this song in worship to the Lord? Now the only question is: *What song are you singing?*

PRAYERS AND CONFESSIONS

A Prayer for Our Government

I Timothy 2:1-2 says that we are to pray, intercede and give thanks for the kings and all people in authority. This is God's command to every believer today. Here is a confession for you to use in prayer for our nation and its leaders. Pray it in faith, believing, and remember God watches over His Word to perform it. (Jeremiah 1:12, *The Amplified Bible*)

"Father, in Jesus' Name, I give thanks for our country and its government. I bring before You the men and women in positions of authority. I pray and intercede for the president, congressmen, senators, judges, policemen, governors, mayors of

our land. I pray for all people in authority over us in any way.

I pray that the Spirit of the Lord rests upon them. I believe that skillful and godly wisdom has entered the heart of our president and knowledge is pleasant to him. Discretion watches over him; understanding keeps him and delivers him from the way of evil and from evil men.

Father, I ask You to encompass the president with men and women who make their hearts and ears attentive to godly counsel and who do that which is right in Your sight. I believe You cause them to be men and women of integrity, who are obedient concerning us. I believe that they lead us in a quiet and peaceable life in all godliness and honesty.

Your Word declares, "Blessed is the nation whose God is the Lord." I receive Your Blessing and declare with my mouth that Your people dwell safely in this land, and they prosper abundantly. It is written in Your Word that the heart of the king is in the hand of the Lord and that You turn it whichever way You desire. I believe the heart of our leader is in Your hand and that his decisions are divinely directed of the Lord. I give thanks unto You that the good news of the Gospel is published in our land. The Word of the Lord prevails and grows mightily in the hearts and lives of the people. I give thanks for this land and the leaders you have given to us, in Jesus' Name. I proclaim that Jesus is Lord over the United States of America!

Prayer References: I Timothy 2:1-2; Proverbs 2:11-12, The Amplified Bible; Psalms 33:12; Proverbs 21:1

A Prayer for Our Schools

More than 44 million students are enrolled in the United States' public schools. They are instructed by 2.6 million teachers. * These numbers certainly justify a tremendous spiritual outreach and call to intercessory prayer. What are we contending for? The souls, the lives and the futures of the upcoming generations. Today's educational system had drastically separated from what God first established in this nation through leaders who sought His counsel. The Word of God once served as the basic element in educating Americans. The Ten Commandments were even displayed in schools as a guide to moral attitude and conduct. The state of our educational system may look hopeless, but when something looks hopeless, it is evidence of a spiritual problem. Hope can begin to work in these circumstances. **Hope** is a spiritual force which grows stronger and stronger the longer we stand. **Faith** can begin to work in these circumstances. "Now faith is the substance of things, hoped for, the evidence of things not seen" (Hebrews 11:1). **Patience** can begin to work in these circumstances. The definition of patience is being constant or being always the same. As believers exercise these three spiritual forces, the Word of God can work to change the direction of American education. Our

God is a good God! He caused the captivity of Judah and Israel to be reversed, then rebuilt them as they were at first (Jeremiah 33:7). He can do the same in our schools. Pray this prayer of faith and set yourself in agreement with the Word of God for the restoration of God's principles in all levels of education.

"Almighty God, I set myself in agreement with the Word of God and with what You once established in American education. I release my hope and faith in your Word. I patiently expect Your Glory to be manifest in schools all across our nation. I come before You on behalf of the students, educators, and administrators of the

entire educational system in America. Lord Jesus, I ask you to restore honor, integrity, virtue, and peace in American classrooms. I confess Isaiah 54:13: 'All thy children shall be taught of the Lord; and great shall be the peace of thy children.' Every time I hear a report of violence and terror in our schools, I will say out loud, "Our children are taught of the Lord and great is the peace and the Anointing upon them!" Jesus, You and I know the educators and the administrators cannot teach and run our schools without You and Your Anointing. So, I intercede and give thanks for those You have ordained and placed in positions of authority and responsibility in our schools across America. I believe for Your Anointing to be in them and upon them.

I am not waiting until I see the Spirit of God moving in this situation. I am starting my confession NOW! I combine my faith with those who are praying and believing for the wisdom, and honor, power, and Glory of God to be demonstrated in our school system. I am releasing my faith for the next generation! Lord Jesus, I thank You for the redemptive work You are doing in our schools and in the people who run them. The students and teachers are on Your heart, and they are on mine, too. Our schools will be a joy, a praise and a glory before all the nations of the earth! Nations will fear God and tremble because of all the goodness, peace, prosperity, security and stability You have provided in Jesus!"

*National Center for Education Statistics Report, May 1996

A Prayer for Revival

Waves of revival have swept around the world in the 20th Century. Today, the five largest churches in the world are Spirit-filled and growing daily. Spirit-filled Christians are increasing in great numbers, as worldwide revival brings the life of God to the church and to all mankind. The Hebrew word for revive is **chayah** which means *to live, have life, remain alive, sustain life, nourish, and preserve life, live prosperously, live forever, be quickened, be alive, be restored to life and health.*

According to that definition, revival is not just a one-time shot of life. Revival is a continual nourishment, preservation, quickening and restoration to life. Revival begins when people return to God. It breaks forth from intercessory prayer and continues when people repent and no longer tolerate sin in their lives.

After Jesus ascended to heaven, the disciples returned to the upper room and continued in daily prayer, in one accord, and in one place. Then, at the appointed time, the Holy Spirit burst onto the scene with the sound of a mighty rushing wind. Peter and the others received God's long-awaited promise of the Holy Spirit's anointing. Acts 2:17-19 repeats the prophecy of Joel, *"And it shall come to pass in the last days, says God, That I will pour out my spirit in those days, And they shall prophesy... I will show wonders in heaven above and signs in the earth beneath..."* (New King James Version).

As they moved out into the streets from the upper room, men from every part of the world saw and heard something different. Peter's great sermon, preached under the anointing of God, brought understanding, conviction of sin and the life of God to those who heard and responded in faith. Prayer, the anointed preaching of the Word, and a supernatural move of God all working together brought revival---God's life-giving power. Oh, what a time to live in! Destruction and despair may be on one hand, but revival and miracles are on the other. Revival is spontaneous and ongoing. It happens when the Spirit of God moves among the people. God never intended for the revival to stop. That is why it is so important to be ready and available as God moves and pours our His Spirit. He can minister life at any moment, to one or to a multitude, to a person in a barren wilderness or to many people in a crowded city.

Revival happens whenever the Word of God prevails. Miracles, signs, and wonders happen wherever the Word of God prevails. Hearts and lives are changed wherever the Word of God prevails. The Bible says ...*God working with them and confirming His word with signs following* (Mark 16:20).

As we look in the Word of God, it is life to us; and revival will come and remain. Revival will become an ongoing way of life. As you set yourself in agreement with God's Will for revival, pray the following prayer or one similar, expecting God to move.

"Father God, because you care for Your people and want all mankind to have life, You desire revival. Your revival brings life and nourishment, preservation and restoration. Thank you for sending Jesus to give us Your abundant life Lord, start a revival in me first. I am Your servant and I place myself in position to receive revival. I feed on the Scriptures as a sheep feeds in green pastures, because Your words are life to me.

Holy Spirit of God, You raised Jesus from the dead, and You dwell in me. So, I yield to You to energize my spirit, restore my soul, and rejuvenate my mortal body. I renew my mind with Your Word. In my innermost being is a well of living water and I am revived! Revival not only is life to me, but life to everyone who calls on the Name of the Lord. Therefore, I intercede on behalf of the people. I call upon You as the God of Abraham, Isaac, and Jacob I call upon the mighty Name of Jesus. All of mankind needs life, Lord! All of mankind needs revival because it is life- Your life.

I speak and sow seeds of revival everywhere I go. I send forth angels to reap the harvest of revival all over the world. I put my hand to the sickle to reap the rich harvest of revival in my home, my church, my community, in the marketplace, on the job, in my country and in all the world. Pour Yourself out on the people. Lord of the harvest, send forth laborers, positioning them in strategic places to minister as You pour out Your Spirit on all flesh. Almighty God, show Yourself mighty and strong with signs and wonders. Holy Spirit, breathe on all the people of the world. I pray this in the Name above all names, Jesus. Amen."

Prayer references: John 3:16-17, 10:10; Proverbs 4:20-22; John 6:63; Romans 8:11; Ephesians 4:23-24; Colossians 3:10; John 4:14, 7:38; Mathew 13:39, 9:38; II Chronicles 16:9; Romans 15:19

Understanding Redemption

God is able to establish us in the faith according to the plan of redemption which had been hidden over the ages. After the Fall in the Garden of Eden, God spoke and outlined the plan. What He laid down put Satan out of business completely. Praise God! He has commanded that the plan of redemption be revealed to His people by His Word. This outline will help you, step by step, understand the reality of it and prevent Satan from lording over you.

1. **The Plan of Redemption called for an Incarnation** (The Union of Divinity with Humanity in Jesus Christ).

Man was the key figure in the Fall. Therefore, it took a man, Jesus, to be the key figure in the redemption of man. When we were born into this world, ruled by Satan, we did not naturally know God. Therefore, the objective of the incarnation is that men may be given the right to become sons of God by receiving the nature of God (John 1:12-13; II Peter 1:3-4).

2. **Redemption Comes from Knowledge.**

God's divine power has already provided everything that pertains to life and godliness. You can escape from the corruption in the world and partake of the divine nature of God. And you can have peace and grace multiplied to you through the knowledge of God and of Jesus our Lord (I Peter 1:1-4). It's there for you! But this revelation knowledge is not sense knowledge, doctrine, philosophies, and creeds. It is the reality and full truth of the Word of God revealed by the Holy Spirit (James 3:13-18). Revelation knowledge is literally knowledge brought to you by revelation!

3. **Satan's Lordship Has Been Broken.**

Revelation 12:11 tells us that the believers overcome by the blood of the lamb and by the word of their testimony, or confession. Confession brings possession. Boldly confess, *"I am an overcomer by the blood of the Lamb and by the word of my testimony. I am redeemed from the lordship of Satan. I can stop his assignments every time."* (II Corinthians 10:4; James 4:7). Satan is not the head of the Church. Jesus is the Head of the Church (Ephesians 4:15-16, 5:23; Colossians 1:18, 2:10). Satan has no rule over you. Hallelujah!

4. **You Are Bought With A Price.**

I Corinthians 6:19-20 tells us we are the temple of the Holy Spirit, which is received from God. This means that we don't own ourselves. We were bought with a price paid through the plan of redemption. Because of that, we should glorify God in our bodies and spirits.

5. **God's Response.**

When you begin to take your place and assume your rights and privileges in Christ, then God begins to respond to you. The Word gives us our inheritance (Acts 20:32; Colossians 1:12). As you study the scriptures in this outline, our prayer is that you come to the full knowledge of who you are in Christ, especially in light of the redemption plan. God will bless you! Amen!

Understanding Confession

Words are spiritual, they carry power. The words we speak are of vital importance to our lives. Jesus said, *"I say unto you, that every idle word that men shall speak, they shall give account thereof in the day of judgment. For by thy words thou shalt be justified, and by thy words thou shalt be condemned"* (Matthew 12:36-37).

When God created the human race, he placed in us the special ability to choose our own words and speak them forth at will. That ability makes the human being different from all other creatures, even the angels. Angels can speak but they can only speak the words God tells them to speak. They act, but only by the command of God.

Man's unique ability to choose and speak words has become a key factor in the development of the human race. Proverbs 12:14 tells us that we shall be satisfied with good by the fruit of our mouths. In Matthew 12:34, Jesus said, *"...out of the abundance of the heart the mouth speaketh."*

If we are not enjoying the reality of God's Word, it is because our confession has us bound. Confession of the Word of God isn't lying, for what we must realize is that we are not trying to get God to do anything. The benefits God has given us in His Word are ours already and Satan is trying to steal them!

So confessing isn't lying. It's a statement of truth. If you didn't know Jesus bore your sickness and disease and told someone you were healed because of your own merits, then you would be lying. But to tell someone that you are healed because the Bible says, *"by His stripes you were healed,"* is speaking the truth that Jesus has already redeemed you from the curse of the law (Deuteronomy 28; Galatians 3:13).

Here are five basic confessions for you to use so that you can enjoy all that God has for you:

1. **Jesus is My Lord.** Philippians 2:9-11

"I confess the complete lordship of Jesus Christ. Jesus is Lord over all, and He has given me authority. As I confess Him, His Word and His Name, and resist Satan in His Name, Satan must bow His knee."

2. **I Do Not Have A Care.** I Peter 5:7; Psalms 37:23-24

"I cast all my care on Jesus because He cares for me. He upholds me as He guides my steps."

3. **I Do Not Want.** Psalms 23:1; Philippians 4:19

"The Lord is my Shepherd. I shall not want. For my God supplies all my need according to His riches in glory by Christ Jesus.

4. **I Am Free from Sin, Sickness, Sorrow, Grief and Fear.** Isaiah 53:3-5; Matthew 8:17; I Peter 2:24

"Every sin, sickness, disease, sorrow and grief was laid on Jesus so that I could be free from them. Therefore, today I am forgiven, healed, healthy and well. I live in divine health."

5. **Jesus is made unto me Wisdom, Righteousness, Sanctification and Redemption.** I Corinthians 1:30; Colossians 2:10

"I confess that Jesus is my wisdom, righteousness, sanctification, and redemption. Only in Him am I entirely complete."

Continue to change your circumstances by filling your heart with the Word of God. Confess these truths and other scriptures so that the words that come out of your mouth are life-changing words. Let your word be God's Word!

A Confession to Walk in the Anointing

I give God praise for His anointing. I thank God because His grace is always sufficient for me. He gives me confidence to face each moment. I believe and confess that the anointing of the Holy Spirit, that remove bondages and destroys yokes, resides in and on me. Through me, the joy of the Lord is released to those who lack it. I am anointed to subdue nations for God. The power of God resides in me to withstand the evil gadgets of the enemy.

By faith I confess that the anointing of God makes the difference in my life and ministry. I am anointed to bring good tidings to those who are in need and set free people from emotional prisons. I am a prophetic voice to my generation. The word of the Lord in my mouth shall always be anointed.

The songs that I sing to the Lord will always be anointed. I am blessed and highly favored.

Thank you that your glory rests upon my life and ministry. I am a vessel that carries the anointing of the Holy Spirit. The fruits and gifts of the Holy Spirit flow through me. For there are diversities of operations and different administrations but the same Lord. The manifestation of the Holy Spirit is given to me to profit others. Thank you, Father, that the Holy Spirit works through me and has divided to me and every man the manifestations of the Holy Spirit.

I covet the best gifts and the manifestation of each to be evident in my life: the word of wisdom, knowledge, faith, gifts of healing, the working of miracles, prophecy, discerning of spirits, diverse kinds of tongues, and the interpretation of tongues. I do not walk in the flesh. I walk in the Spirit. I do not fulfill the lusts of the flesh; and the fruit of the spirit are evident in my life and ministry to others. For the fruit of the Spirit is love, joy, peace, long-suffering, gentleness, goodness, faith, meekness, temperance: against such there is no law.

I am baptized into Christ by the Holy Spirit and Jesus has baptized me in the Holy Ghost and power. I am anointed to do good healing all who are oppressed of the devil. I am spiritually trained, and my senses are trained to discern good from evil. I worship and flow in the Holy Spirit; and He reveals the will of the Father to me in every circumstance and in every situation. I am a sheep. I hear His voice and the voice of a stranger I will not follow.

I am born again. I have been joined to Almighty God. I am a partaker of God's divine nature. His divine power has given to me everything that I need that pertains to life and godliness through the knowledge that has called us to glory and virtue. I have been given a new heart and a new Spirit.

I am anointed. I am consecrated: devoted and set apart for the worship and service of God. I am sanctified: purified and productive with spiritual blessings for God's holy purposes. I have a life full of components that all work together for my good. I am crucified with Christ and consider my life and all things that I possess as trash for the sake of the cross and to carry the glory of God. The cost of my anointing is expensive and valuable. I endure the cross and come out above only and never beneath. Regardless of what I have gone through, I have a joyful aroma that perfumes the air while I am growing. I am a blessing to those around me and closest to me. The hopes and dreams inside of me are manifesting. I am filled with the Holy Spirit. I am moving in a fresh anointing. I am experiencing the promises of God. I am a visionary and a dreamer. I prophesy and declare God's Word. I call on the name of the Lord and I am saved in every situation.

I am anointed to cast out demons. I am anointed to speak with new tongues. I am anointed to overcome deadly situations. I am anointed to lay hands on the sick and they recover. I am anointed to be a witness for Christ and share my testimony. I am anointed be an ambassador of Christ; a duplicate of Christ, representing Him in the earth. I am anointed to change circumstances around me. I am anointed with trailblazing skills. I am anointed with time-management skills. I am anointed to get the wealth to establish God's covenant in the Earth. I am anointed to manage wealth. I am anointed for debt-free living. I am anointed to train, and I am anointed to reign. I am anointed to worship and praise. I have grace to serve. I am anointed to receive divine favor and Kingdom strategies. I am anointed to prosper. I am anointed to attract blessings. I am anointed to be a blessing today in Jesus' Name. Amen.

A Confession of Praise and Worship

Father, in the Name of Jesus, we give thanks unto you Lord. We enter your gates with thanksgiving; and enter your courts with praise. With the lifting of our hands, with the lifting of our voices, on the stringed instruments, we celebrate your Name. We call upon your Name. Hallowed be your Name. For the Lord is good and His mercy endureth forever! Hallelujah! You are Holy and we glory in your Holy Name. You are worthy Lord! You are mighty Father! We make known your mighty deeds among the people. We remember your great works. Let the hearts of those that seek you rejoice!

We seek you first, your Kingdom and Your righteousness and we receive answers every time we do. Through our praising, our playing, we prophesy of your goodness. We praise and worship you under the inspiration of the Holy Spirit. We let your praise continually be on our lips. As we (vocalists and instrumentalist alike) unify and make one sound to be heard, we lift up our sound; and as we lift up our voices with the instruments of music, your presence fills the temple. Hallelujah! The Glory of the Lord fills the house, and we get answers from your throne! We praise the beauty of your holiness Lord. We sound with all of creation, with the angels in Heaven. Holy! Holy! Holy is the Lord! Worthy! You are worthy to receive honor and glory! For your deliver us! You are our protector. You are our God. So, we stand to every morning and every evening to boast forth your praise. We are priests of praise: a chosen generation, a royal priesthood, a holy Nation, a peculiar people who are in love with shewing forth your praise. We sing mightily unto you Lord each day, even in our secret places of worship with gladness of heart, bowing our heads and hearts in personal worship and devotion to you.

As we call upon you, faithful God, thank you for saving us from our enemies. Thank you for crowning us every morning with lovingkindness and giving us the wisdom that require of you. We trust in you. We lean not to our own understanding. We acknowledge you in all our ways. We ask you for wisdom as we worship you All Mighty God- in spirit and in truth. For you have declared that whoso offereth praise glorifieth you; and to him that ordereth his conversation aright will you show all the benefits of your salvation (Ps 50:14). You hath put a new song in my mouth even a praise song unto our God. You give me wisdom every time I pray.

I believe I receive wisdom. I have the mind of Christ. The Holy Spirit shews me the things that are freely given unto me from God. I will not allow any vain imaginations, negative thoughts and emotions to in any way influence me. I take every thought captive to the obedience of Christ. I rebuke the spirit of heaviness and command it to depart from my presence. You have given me the garment of praise for the Spirit of heaviness. All things are possible for me because I believe. I worship you and fully agree with your Word. I cancel any covenant, promise, pact, oath, agreement or contract I may have entered into knowingly or unknowingly, willingly or unwillingly that was anything other than the covenant of Jesus Christ.

Father, I choose to fix my eyes upon You as You have commanded. I choose to look for direction and understanding from you. I choose to honor vision. I choose to ask for vision and direction. I will honor your direction. I am a believer. I believe the Bible works for me! God speaks to me. I choose anointed reason over my own reasoning. I choose revelation knowledge over Earthly knowledge. I am brilliant because I yield my reasoning capacity to the flow of the Holy Spirit. I let the Holy Spirit guide my reasoning capacity. I choose to be brilliant all the time; so, I choose to be humble and give God the glory for the brilliance that flows through me. This is my decision.

So, hold not thy peace, O God of my praise song. Sing over me, dance over me. Compass me about with songs of deliverance. Speak to our hearts. Take joy in us. Renew us in your love. You are making a song of joy over me. I welcome the

Holy Spirit to use my voice and begin to sing through me. His praises shall continually be in my mouth!! The praises of the Holy Spirit shall continually be in my mouth!! You are in our midst. You inhabit the praises of your people- celebrating over us with singing. You're in our midst- a warrior who can deliver. We are humbled by the fact that the God who created the Heavens and the Earth takes great delight in us. Thank You, Father in Jesus' Name. Amen!

Prayer References: 2 Sam 22:50; I Chron. 16:8-12,41-42; 23:30; 2 Chron. 5:13; 2 Chron. 20:21; 29:30; Isa. 42:10; 43:21; Zeph. 3:17; Ps 7:17; 34:1; 40:3; 100:14; 199:1; John 4:23; 1 Pet. 2:9

YOUR OPPORTUNITY TO PARTNER

Partnership is dynamic. But partnership is not a one-sided relationship. As the Apostle Paul said, *"I thank my God upon every remembrance of you... For your fellowship in the gospel from the first day until now... because I have you in my heart; inasmuch as both in my bonds, and in the defense and confirmation of the gospel, ye are all partakers of my grace* (Philippians 1:3, 5,7)." Paul was saying "I have you in my heart, I'm praying for you and I'm not going to let you fail!" His partners had become a major part of his ministry. They fought alongside him in prayer, they ministered to his needs, and provided for other ministers that he sent to help build them spiritually. That's how partnership works.

The partners have a significant role in this ministry. God provides for the ministry through them: through their prayers, words of encouragement, support, and through their giving to what God is doing through the ministry. And every day we see and hear of the great rewards they are receiving as a result of their partnership. If God is directing you to become a partner, or if you are already a partner, press in to get a revelation of God's will for you, and then get ready for the adventure and rewards that come when you release the power of partnership in your life.

The Blessing of the Twice Sown Seed

"And he...took the five loaves, and two fishes, and looking up toward heaven he blessed, and brake, and gave the loaves to his disciples, and the disciples to the multitude. And they did all eat and were filled: and they took up of the fragments that remained twelve baskets full. And they that had eaten were about five thousand men beside women and children" (Matthew 14:19-21).

When you support Singleness of Heart Ministries International, your giving stretches further than the lives we can touch. It stretches from orphanages to healing ministries to evangelical meetings to medical teams. We reach all over the globe through the principle of the twice-sown seed.

When you give, a minimum of 10 percent of every gift is given to other ministries that reach people we can't. We actually re-sow a tenth of your gift and product purchases into lives all over the world. And just like the boy who gave his loaves and fish to Jesus, we see the increase on the seed-faith gifts of our partners. Through partnership in ministry, we are reaching greater numbers of people than any of us could reach on our own- people who have no other way to hear the Good News.

We stand with ministries which train and minister through educating, credentialing and assisting men and women in the Word of God, prayer, and divine leadership. We support outreaches who are committed to fulfilling the Great Commission through the preaching and teaching of the Gospel in countries across the world! We also help to provide theological training for ministers and laity alike. We support efforts to develop Bible schools, care for children and orphans, feed the needy, reach the lost, and win souls.

We promote the Gospel through quality Christian television and radio programming that features the works of the Body of Christ, as well as quality preaching, teaching, missions documentaries, testimonials, music, movies, and children programming. People from all walks off life (from inner cities to rural towns) are all among the millions of lives touched by the love of our partners giving.

You enable us to put legs to our prayers by putting substance into our hands to be effective soldiers of the cross. As a result, you will share the reward of this harvest someday! Lives are changed *eternally,* and blessings overflow to the giver! That's the power of partnership. Praise God! That's the power of the twice-sown seed!

Singleness of Heart Ministries

www.SinglenessofHeartMin.org

A PARTNER:
One who shares responsibility in some common activity with another individual or group.

BECOMING A PARTNER

Our Responsibility

- Pray on a daily basis that God's blessing be upon you.

- Provide spiritual and life enrichment resources for you online.

- Bless you with a free gift from time to time (ie. music, downloads, etc.).

- Provide partner conferences, meetings and events online and offline.

- Serve Christ through serving mankind.

Your Responsibility

- Pray for us always.
- Support our outreach efforts, especially in your area.
- Prayerfully sow financially into our outreach efforts.
- Always uplift us with the words that you speak.
- Serve Christ through serving mankind.

Dr. Roz, I want to access the *Power* of this *Anointed Prayer Partnership*!

Sign Up To Become an Official Partner Online:
www.SinglenessofHeartMin.org

Name: _____
Address: _____
Email: _____
Cell: _____ Age: ____ Gender: ☐ M ☐ F

- -

Give To Support: www.PayPal.me/SOHMin
www.SinglenessofHeartMin.org

I want to support with a: ☐ love gift: $ _____
☐ monthly pledge: ☐ $10   ☐ $25   ☐ $50
☐ $100   ☐ 250   ☐ $500   ☐ Other: $ _____
to help you accomplish the vision of winning the lost and encouraging the saints through the Word of God! _____, *Signature*

- -

Leave A Prayer Request &
Sign Up For The Online Study Course:
www.SinglenessofHeartMin.org

Prayer Request: ☐ Salvation ☐ Peace ☐ Healing
☐ Financial Increase ☐ Wisdom/Direction
☐ Other _____

Singleness of Heart Ministries

www.SinglenessofHeartMin.org

SINGLENESS OF HEART MINISTRIES

PRAYER FOR OUR MINISTRY PARTNERS

Father, in the Name of Jesus, we pray to you on behalf of our all of our partners, who pray for us, support our local meetings, cheerfully sow financially into this ministry, and always uplift the ministry, our ministers and their families with the words that they speak. Father, we thank you for our partners and for their service and dedication to serve you. Thank you that they bring forth the fruit of the Spirit: love, joy, peace, long-suffering, gentleness, goodness, faith, meekness, and temperance.

Father, thank you that our partners are good ground, that they hear Your Word and understand it, and that the Word bears fruit in their lives. They are like trees planted by rivers of water that bring forth fruit in its season. Their leaf shall not wither, and whatever they do shall prosper.

From the first day we heard of our partners, we have not stopped praying for them, asking you to give them wise minds and spirits attuned to your will. Our partners are merciful as you, Father, are merciful. They will judge only as they want to be judged. They do not condemn, and they are not condemned. Our partners forgive others and people forgive them. They give and men will give to them- yes, good measure, pressed down, shaken together, running over will they pour into their laps. For whatever measure they bless us with other people will use in their dealings with them. They are generous and lend freely. They conduct their affairs with justice. Lord, Your Word says that surely, they will never be shaken.

Father, we ask you to bless our partners with all spiritual blessings in heavenly places that good will might come to them. They make melody in their hearts as unto you Lord and your glory upon their life and ministry is evident. Anoint them to worship you; and give them answers every time they do. We declare that they are not ignorant of any spiritual gift. The gifts of the Holy Spirit flow effortlessly in them. Father may the same anointing of prophetic worship that rests on this ministry, rest on them. As they worship you, they flow effortlessly in the Spirit of wisdom, knowledge, faith, healing, miracles, prophecy, discerning of spirits, divers kinds of tongues, the interpretation of tongues in Jesus' Name- receiving answers from you every time they do. Give them an ear sensitive to your leading. Give them a voice joyful in praises! Let *your* praises continually be in their mouths. Grant them revelation of the power of worship. Release the high praises of God through their mouths in Jesus' Name.

When they worship let lives be changed! Let bodies be healed! Let the captives be set free!! Restore the mind and bring peace to soul! Let your plans be fulfilled in their lives and we thank you for your mercies on their behalf. In Jesus' Name we pray. Amen.

        Colossians 1:9   Psalm 112:5-9; 147

        Jeremiah 29:11   2 Chronicles 20

Galatians 5   Ephesians 5:19   Corinthians 12

Notes

Notes

Notes

About The Author

Dr. R. Buffer, D.C.E., affectionately known as Dr. Roz, ministers primarily to unmarried women through Singleness of Heart Ministries, a ministry outreach dedicated to teaching young women to live in singleness of heart unto the Lord. Dr. Roz teaches others how this can be practically accomplished in our everyday lives using hymns and sacred music. This is further explained by the ministry motto: *"...Finding Purpose in Him (Hymn)"*.

Dr. Roz is a worship leader, author, businesswoman, and devoted servant to the Body of Christ. Dr. Roz has a *heritage* and *passion* for two main things: *Education* and *the Arts*. As an avid supporter of Christian Education, she has a fervent desire to see young adults won to Christ and actively pursuing fulfilling God's will for their lives. As a daughter of two retired music educators, Dr. Roz has been involved in formal music training for 20+ years. Dr. Roz is a life-changing conference speaker. She is graced to minister on topics that helps one maintain *singleness of heart* such as: purpose, life lessons from hymns, praise, spontaneous worship, the doctrine of Christ, as well as other topics related to the dynamics of music and vocal training.

Her passion is to teach young women to maximize their intimacy with God by hymns, praise, worship, and a lifestyle of purity and excellence. Her practical approach of teaching young women to live in singleness of heart encourages others to pursue and fulfill God's call for their lives. **For other books by Dr. Roz or to enroll in one of her classes, go to www.SinglenessofHeartMin.org today!**

prayerbase.net